Level 2
TECHNIQUE

P9-APG-030

Exploring Piano Classics
A Masterwork Method for the Developing Pianist

NANCY BACHUS

ISBN-10: 0-7390-5554-2
ISBN-13: 978-0-7390-5554-0

Alfred

About the *Exploring Piano Classics* Series

Exploring Piano Classics: A Masterworks Method for Developing Pianists pairs motivating performance repertoire with thoughtful technical studies. Each level contains two books:

■ *Exploring Piano Classics—Repertoire* includes pieces from the major style periods. The repertoire was selected and graded by studying festival, competition, and examination lists from the United States, Canada, and the United Kingdom. Background information on each style period, its instruments, composers, and the music itself is included. The CD performances of the repertoire in each level provide an indispensable auditory learning tool for appropriate musical interpretation.

■ *Exploring Piano Classics—Technique* includes **basic keyboard patterns**—five-finger patterns, scales, chords, cadences, and arpeggios in the major and minor keys found in the *Repertoire* book. These patterns can be developed into a daily warm-up routine for each practice session while expanding the student's technical skills. **Exercises and etudes**, an important feature of the *Technique* book, were chosen and written to develop basic keyboard touches and other necessary technical skills for mastering each piece. Suggestions for efficient practice are also included.

These companion books include a convenient page-by-page correlation, allowing the teacher to assign pages in the *Technique* book that reinforce the music that students are learning in the *Repertoire* book. When used together, the books give students a deep understanding of the art of music, performance practices, and the necessary skills to play the piano with technical ease. The knowledge, skills and joy experienced in the study of music through this series will enrich students throughout their lives.

About the Technique Books

Technique is a skill that can be developed by both athletes and pianists. To succeed in both fields, candidates are required to learn to control muscles through practice, repeat technical skills so that they become automatic motions, and use the habits or skills acquired through practice in performances.

As an **athlete at the piano**, it is necessary that students acquire many technical skills that will enable them to play music. *Exploring Piano Classics—Technique* helps the student establish correct physical habits that will be used when playing pieces at any level.

There are three essential building blocks for a reliable piano technique to review daily at all levels of piano playing:

■ Position of the Body at the Piano

■ Focused Fingertips Balanced on the Keyboard

■ Coordinated Motions of the Hands and Arms

These building blocks are introduced in the Preparatory Level on page 4. As students progress, teachers must continually build upon this foundation at higher levels. The studies included in these *Technique* books provide the basis for such development.

Some teachers will want to assign the correlating pages in *Exploring Piano Classics—Repertoire* and *Technique* books. Other teachers may wish to work straight through the *Technique* books, giving the student a totally structured program of technical development.

CONTENTS

Falling for Beautiful, Rich Tone 4
Slur Groups 4
  Slur Warm-Ups 4
Basic Keyboard Patterns. 5
  Five-Finger Aerobics in Contrary Motion 5
Warm-Up Patterns in C. 6
  Five-Finger Patterns in C 6
  Thumb Slides 7
  *C Major and Harmonic Minor Scales
    with Triads and Inversions* 7
  Broken Triads in C 8
  Scale and Four-Note Broken Chord in C. 9
  Cadence Workout in C 9
Increasing Speed with Slur Groups. 10
  Allegro, Biehl. 10
Loosening Knuckles 11
  Floating, le Carpentier. 11
Wrist Circles. 11
  Allegro, Op. 89, No. 4, Krause 11
Warm-Up Patterns in D. 12
  Five-Finger Patterns in D 12
  Thumb Slides 13
  *D Major and Harmonic Minor Scales
    with Triads and Inversions* 13
  Broken Triads in D. 14
  Scale and Four-Note Broken Chord in D 15
  Cadence Workout in D 15
Changing Meter 16
  Andantino (Excerpt), Stravinsky. 16
Echo Phrases 16
Larger Intervals 17
  Andantino, J. C. Bach 17
Two-Note Slurs and Staccato 17
  Youthful Happiness (Excerpt), Türk. 17
Warm-Up Patterns in F. 18
  Five-Finger Patterns in F. 18
  Thumb Slides 19
  *F Major and Harmonic Minor Scales
    with Triads and Inversions* 19
  Broken Triads in F 20
  Scale and Four-Note Broken Chord in F. 21
  Cadence Workout in F 21
More about Two-Note Slurs 22
  Allegretto in C Major (Excerpt), Neefe 22
The Damper Pedal 23
Creating Different Moods 24
  Walking in Rain/Chase Scene. 24
Cross Hands and Add Damper Pedal 25
  Gymnastics, Op. 17, No. 18, Le Couppey 25

Wrist/Hand Staccato. .26
  Skipping 26
Warm-Up Patterns in G. 27
  Five-Finger Patterns in G 27
  Thumb Slides 28
  *G Major and Harmonic Minor Scales
    with Triads and Inversions* 28
  Broken Triads in G 29
  Scale and Four-Note Broken Chord in G 30
  Cadence Workout in G 30
Two Voices in Both Hands 31
  Stuck on Five and One, Op. 82, No. 25, Gurlitt . . .31
Rotation 32
  Rotation Etude, Beyer. 32
Independent Hands 33
  Scales with Independence 33
A "Singing" Melody. .33
Natural Accents, Slurs, and Motion. 34
  Moderato, Op. 38, No. 5, Hässler. 34
Warm-Up Patterns in A. 35
  Five-Finger Patterns in A 35
  Thumb Slides 36
  *A Major and Harmonic Minor Scales
    with Triads and Inversions* 36
  Broken Triads in A 37
  Scale and Four-Note Broken Chord in A. 38
  Cadence Workout in A 38
Imitation 39
  Canon, Gurlitt. 39
Repeated Chords 40
  Bouncing on the Keys. 40
Chords and Rapid Melodies 40
  Allegro, Gossec. .40
Warm-Up Patterns in E. 41
  Five-Finger Patterns in E 41
  Thumb Slides 42
  *E Major and Harmonic Minor Scales
    with Triads and Inversions* 42
  Broken Triads in E 43
  Scale and Four-Note Broken Chord in E. 44
  Cadence Workout in E 44
Double Notes 45
More Repeated Chords. 46
  Etude in E Major, Op. 17, No. 12, Le Couppey . . .46
Combining Touches 47
  Different Touches. 47
  Allegro assai, Op. 38, No. 16, Hässler 47
Alternating Hands. 48
Melody and Ostinato Bass. 48
  Allegro giocoso 48

Falling for Beautiful, Rich Tone

To create beautiful tone, each finger **falls and settles into the key,** rather than pressing it.

- Suspend the RH wrist with fingers slightly above the key.
- On **each** note of the exercise, lower the **wrist to level.**
- Feel the weight of the arm **flow into the firm nail joint** as the wrist falls to a level playing position.
- Play with the LH two octaves lower than written.

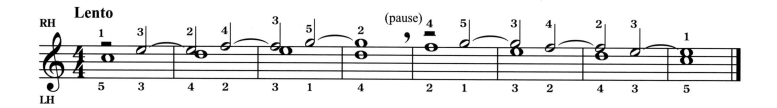

Slur Groups

Slur groups are two or more notes played on one **impulse of energy.**

- **Fall** into the first note as in the above exercise. Feel a center of gravity on each fingertip.
- **Roll** or transfer sideways throughout the slur group.
- The fingertip makes a **graceful release** as the hand closes into a fist.
- Play with the same fingers throughout each line. The LH plays one octave lower.

Slur Warm-Ups

Basic Keyboard Patterns

▦ Place your fingers over the five keys of each five-finger pattern and keep them there.

▦ **Feel** the weight on the nail joint as you fall into the first note of each pattern.

▦ **Roll** from fingertip to fingertip with **legato touch**, and one energy impulse.

▦ Repeat in minor by lowering the third note of each pattern a half step.

Five-Finger Aerobics in Contrary Motion

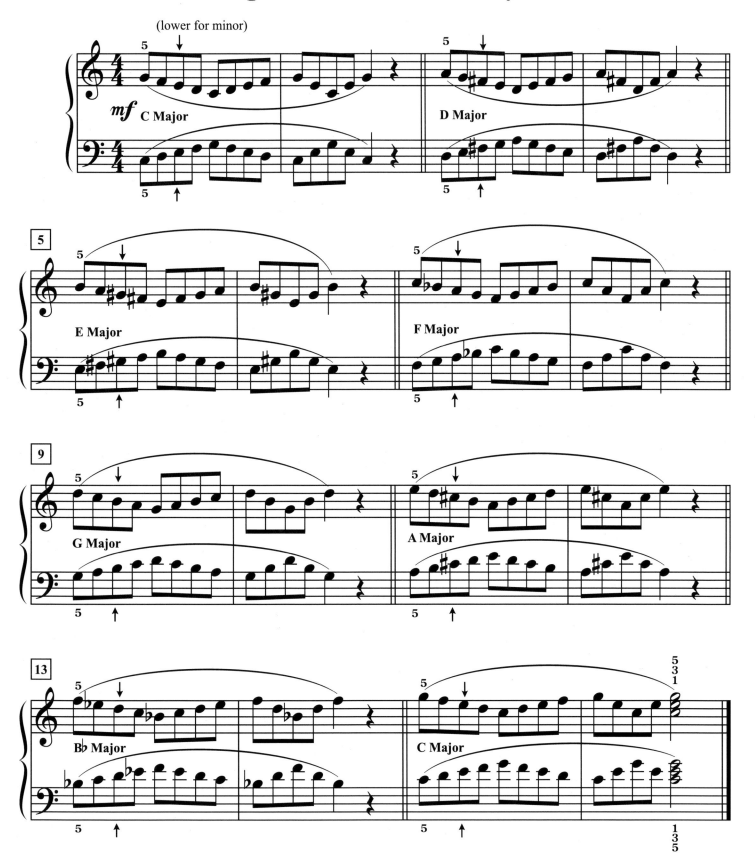

Warm-Up Patterns in C

- ◾ Play mm. 1–3 **three times**, doubling the rhythm on each repeat:
  1) use half notes; 2) quarter notes; 3) eighth notes.

- ◾ Hold the whole notes throughout each measure (mm. 5–8).

- ◾ Make a fist to release all staccato chords (mm. 13–15).

- ◾ Play in minor by lowering the thirds of each pattern a half step.

Five-Finger Patterns in C

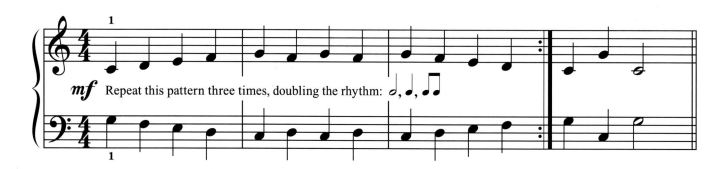

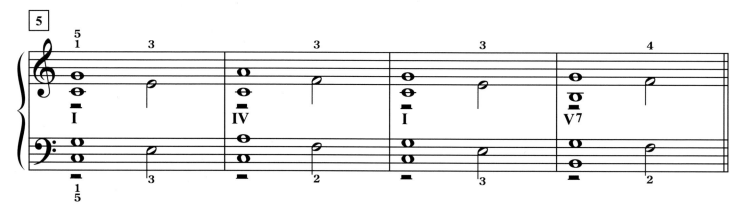

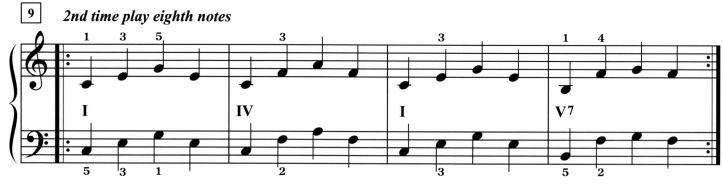

2nd time play eighth notes

("Fist" release on each staccato chord)

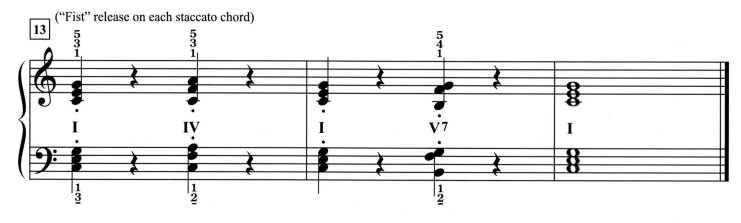

- When playing scales, slide finger 1 under fingers 2 and 3 with **no wrist turns.**
- Play hands separately, with increasing speed.

Thumb Slides

- Play scales with the metronome, making the eighth notes exactly twice as fast as the quarters.
- After playing each chord, **relax** the wrist and forearms, keeping the **nail joints firm**.
- First, play hands separately, then together.

C Major and Harmonic Minor Scales with Triads and Inversions

- Play hands separately, LH two octaves lower than written.
- Position the **fingers over the keys** of the pattern **on the first note** of each triplet group.
- Also play in C minor by lowering all E's a half step.

Broken Triads in C

Scale and Four-Note Broken Chord in C

Open the hand over the keys of the four-note broken chords (mm. 2–4).

- After each blocked chord, **relax the knuckles,** keeping the keys down and the **nail joints firm.**

- Play with the RH one octave higher than written.

- Repeat in minor by lowering all E's and A's a half step.

Cadence Workout in C

10

Increasing Speed with Slur Groups

To play rapidly, group several notes in **one motion**.

Three-Note Slur Groups

Fall from slightly suspended wrist to level on each note.

■ With fingers slightly above the keys, drop on the first note of each slur group.

■ Play the slur in **one motion** of the arm as the fingers rapidly play the other notes.

Picking Up the Pace

■ Begin at a comfortable metronome tempo.

■ Set the metronome four points higher and repeat.

■ Continue until the tempo is challenging.

Allegro

Albert Biehl
(1836–1899)

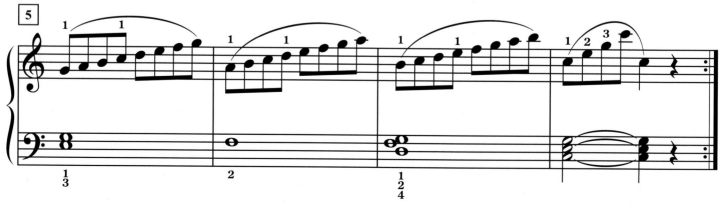

Loosening Knuckles

Keeping knuckles joints loose allows the arm to **float forward**.

▪ Balance on fingers 3-4-5 in both hands.

▪ Keeping the knuckle joints loose and flexible, rock forward and backwards.

Floating

Originally written in ¾ time.

Adolphe Clair le Carpentier
(1809–1869)

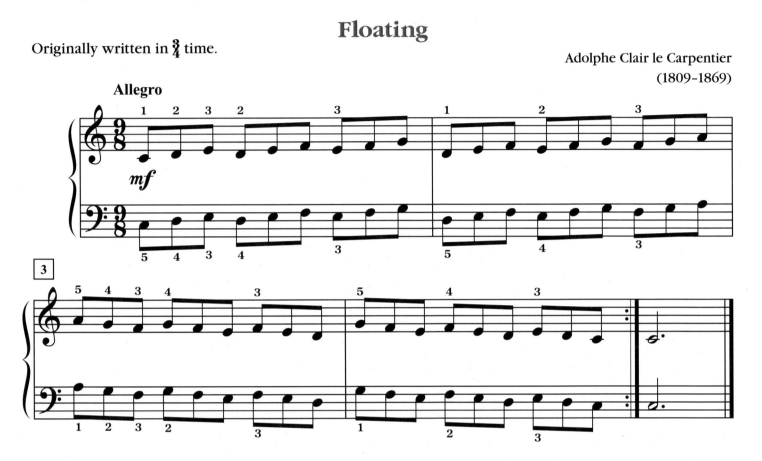

Wrist Circles

Melody in C, p. 7

▪ When playing *Allegro*, align your left forearm with fingers 2 and 3, and allow the left wrist to make small, clockwise circular motions. Knuckles should remain loose.

▪ Play the RH as large slur groups, shaping the melody as you would sing it.

▪ Melodic lines usually crescendo as they ascend and diminuendo as they descend.

Allegro

Anton Krause (1834–1907)
Op. 89, No. 4

Warm-Up Patterns in D

■ Play mm. 1–3 **three times**, doubling the rhythm on each repeat:
1) use half notes; 2) quarter notes; 3) eighth notes.

■ Hold the whole notes throughout each measure (mm. 5–8).

■ Make a fist to release all staccato chords (mm. 13–15).

■ Play in minor by lowering the thirds of each pattern a half step.

Five-Finger Patterns in D

- Balance on RH fingers 2 and 3 and LH fingers 3 and 2.
  Hold the whole notes throughout the exercise.

- Slide the thumb under without turning the wrist.

Thumb Slides

- Play scales with the metronome, making the eighth notes exactly twice as fast as the quarters.

- After playing each chord, **relax** the wrist and forearms, keeping the **nail joints firm.**

- First, play hands separately, then together.

D Major and Harmonic Minor Scales
with Triads and Inversions

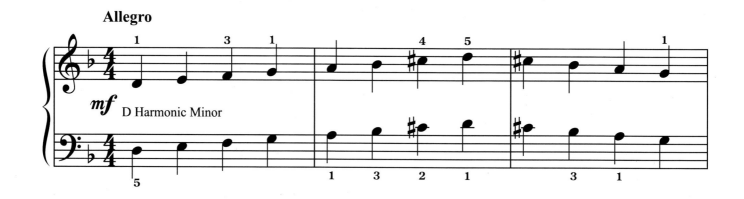

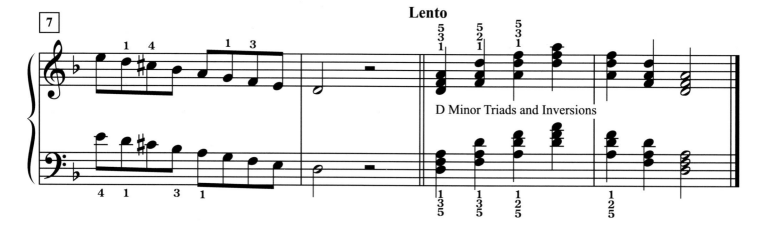

- Play hands separately, LH two octaves lower than written.
- Position the **fingers over the keys** of the pattern **on the first note** of each triplet group.
- Also play in D minor by lowering all F♯'s a half step.

Broken Triads in D

Scale and Four-Note Broken Chord in D

Open the hand over the keys of the four-note broken chords (mm. 2–4).

- After each blocked chord, **relax the knuckles,** keeping the keys down and the **nail joints firm.**
- Play with the RH one octave higher than written.
- Repeat in minor by lowering all F♯'s and B's a half step.

Cadence Workout in D

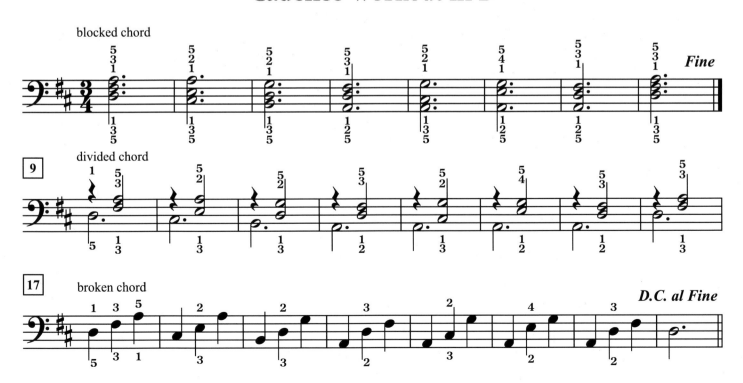

Old English Air, p. 8

Changing Meter

When the meter changes from **2/4** to **3/4**, the ♩ has the same value in both meters. Keep it steady.

Andantino
(Excerpt)

Igor Stravinsky
(1882–1971)

Echo Phrases

Old English Air, p. 8

In early music when a motive or phrase is repeated it is usually played softly on the repeat.

- ■ To play **softly** bring the palm of the hand close to the keyboard, which lowers the wrist. Play with firm fingertips to the bottom of the keys.

- ■ To **crescendo** gradually bring the wrist up to level (normal playing position) and **relax** the arms into the fingertips. More finger action also helps increase sound.

Larger Intervals

It is important to **feel** larger intervals without looking at the keyboard.

■ Open the hand from the **knuckle of finger 5** to the curved **nail joint of finger 1.**

■ Move the forearm horizontally to play the intervals.

Andantino

Two-Note Slurs and Staccato

Rustic Dance, p. 10, *Minuet in C Minor*, p. 11

A two-note slur followed by a detached or staccato note is common in Baroque- and Classical-style music.

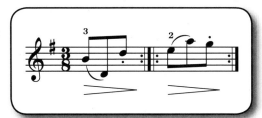

■ Play the two-note slur with a release so that there is a separation between the last note of the slur and the following note.

■ Other eighth notes not marked with a slur are played slightly detached.

Youthful Happiness
(Excerpt)

Johann Gottlob Türk
(1750–1813)

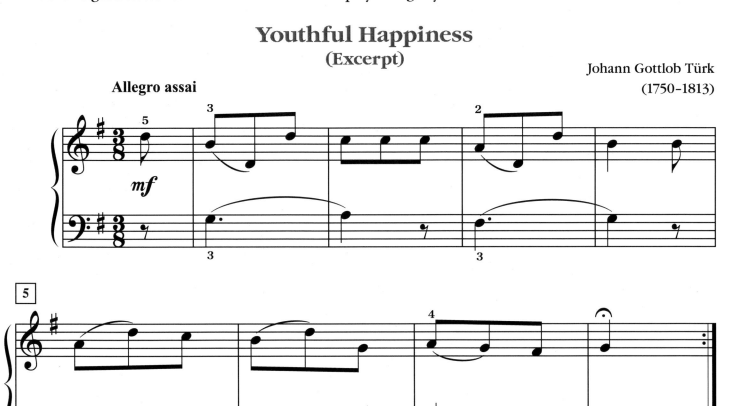

Warm-Up Patterns in F

- Play mm. 1–3 **three times**, doubling the rhythm on each repeat:
  1) use half notes; 2) quarter notes; 3) eighth notes.

- Hold the whole notes throughout each measure (mm. 5–8).

- Make a fist to release all staccato chords (mm. 13–15).

- Play in minor by lowering the thirds of each pattern.

Five-Finger Patterns in F

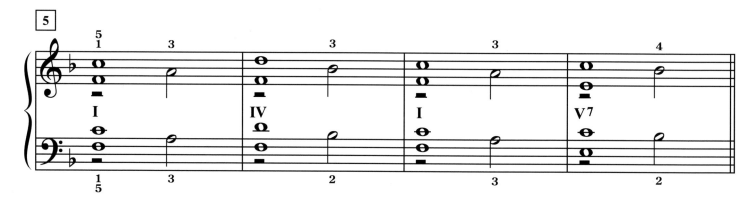

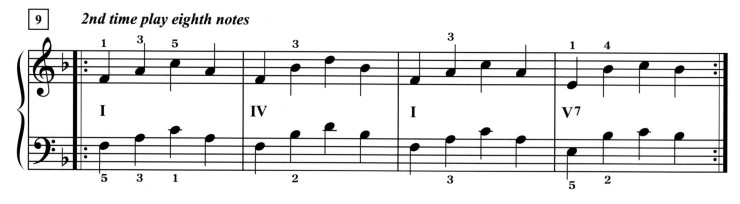

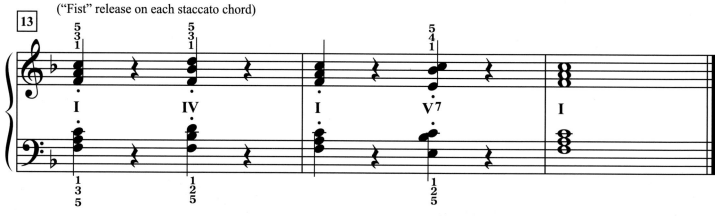

- When playing scales, slide finger 1 under fingers 2 and 3 with **no wrist turns.**

- Play hands separately, with increasing speed.

Thumb Slides

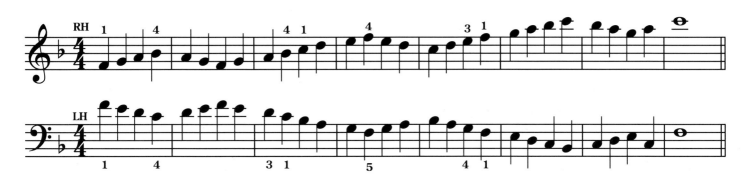

- Play scales with the metronome, making the eighth notes exactly twice as fast as the quarters.

- After playing each chord, **relax** the wrist and forearms, keeping the **nail joints firm.**

- First, play hands separately, then together.

F Major and Harmonic Minor Scales with Triads and Inversions

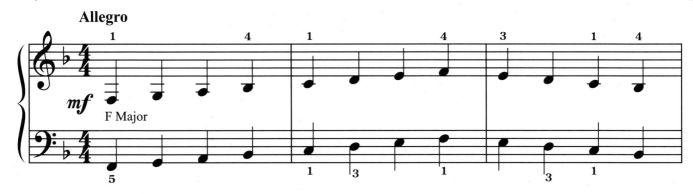

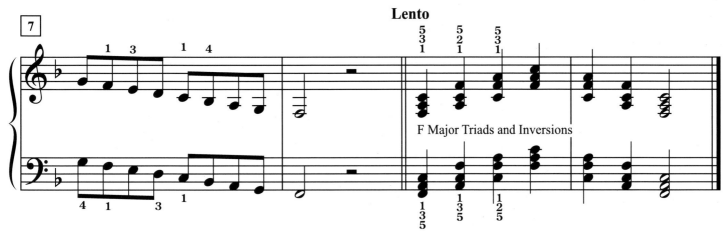

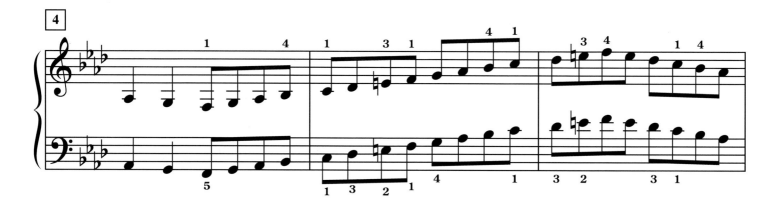

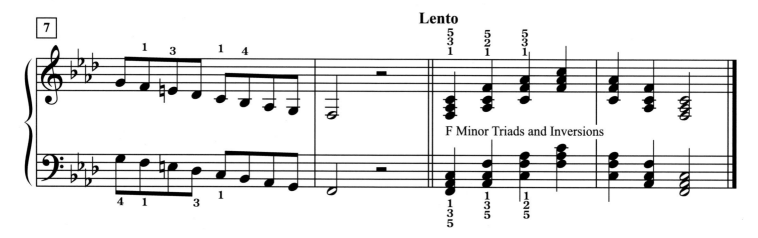

- Play hands separately, LH two octaves lower than written.

- Position the **fingers over the keys** of the pattern **on the first note** of each triplet group.

- Also play in F minor by lowering all A's a half step.

Broken Triads in F

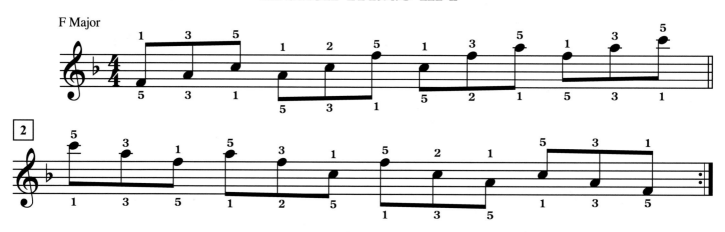

Scale and Four-Note Broken Chord in F

Open the hand over the keys of the four-note broken chords (mm. 2–4).

- After each blocked chord, **relax the knuckles**, keeping the keys down and the **nail joints firm**.
- Play with the RH one octave higher than written.
- Repeat in minor by lowering all A's and D's a half step.

Cadence Workout in F

More about Two-Note Slurs

In most two-note slurs:

- The **first note is fuller** than the second since falling gives it more weight.

- The **second note is shorter** than written as it is released.

- The first note has a feeling of **tension that is resolved** on the second note.

- On each two-note slur: **Fall** on the first note—**transfer** to the next fingertip—**release** gracefully.

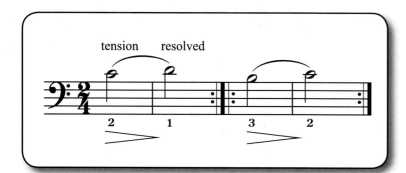 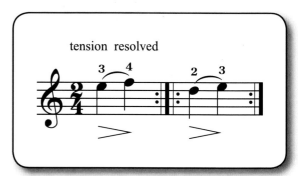

Allegretto in C Major
(Excerpt)

Christian Gottlob Neefe
{1748–1798}

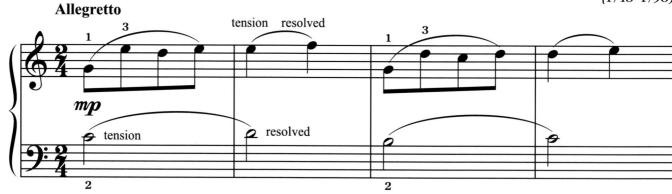

The Damper Pedal

The right, or damper pedal, is used to **enrich, connect, or sustain** tones already struck.
Since the dampers are moved up, the strings vibrate freely.

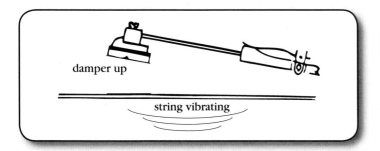

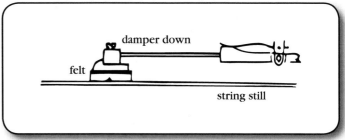

To raise the dampers from the strings:

- ■ Place the heel of the right foot directly behind the damper pedal.
- ■ Place the ball of the foot on the pedal.
- ■ With heel on the floor and foot on the pedal, move the foot silently up and down from the ankle.

Practice moving the foot up and down many times without playing, **saying**:

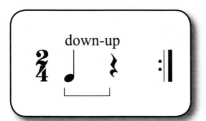

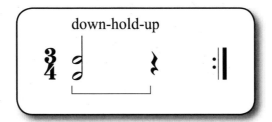

Direct Pedaling

The pedal is moved up and down exactly as the notes are played and released.

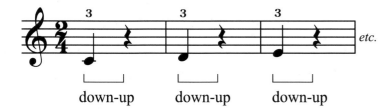

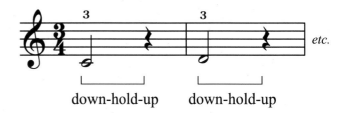

Legato Pedaling

The pedal is pressed down right after striking
a note and changed (moved up and down)
quickly so the sound continues. LISTEN!
No blurs!

24

Creating Different Moods

Different moods can be created by the way we feel and interpret music.

Left-Hand Melody

■ Play the LH melody of *Walking in Rain/Chase Scene* using direct
and legato pedal, listening carefully to avoid blurs.

■ Shape the melody: crescendo as the notes ascend and diminuendo as they descend.

Right-Hand Repeated Chords

■ First play at a moderate **walking** (*Andante*) tempo.
Keep **fingers on the keys,** playing as legato as possible at a quiet dynamic level.

■ Create a murmuring, blended sound (like a **gentle rain**) as background for the LH melody.

■ Finally, create a **chase scene** by playing at a faster (*Allegro*) tempo,
and using a **knocking** motion from the wrist.

Walking in Rain/Chase Scene

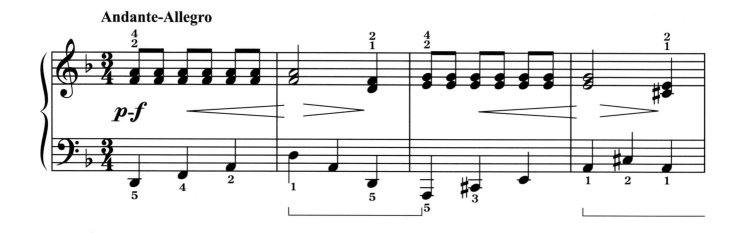

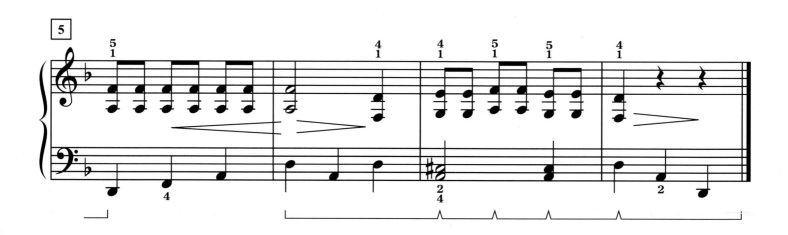

Cross Hands and Add Damper Pedal

- Keeping elbows in one place, move each hand and forearm in arcs or half circles.

- Block the chords, crossing hands in an **arc-like motion**.

- Use the energy of the release of a note to carry you precisely to the next one.

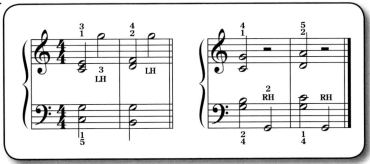

Gymnastics

Félix Le Couppey (1811–1887)
Op. 17, No. 18

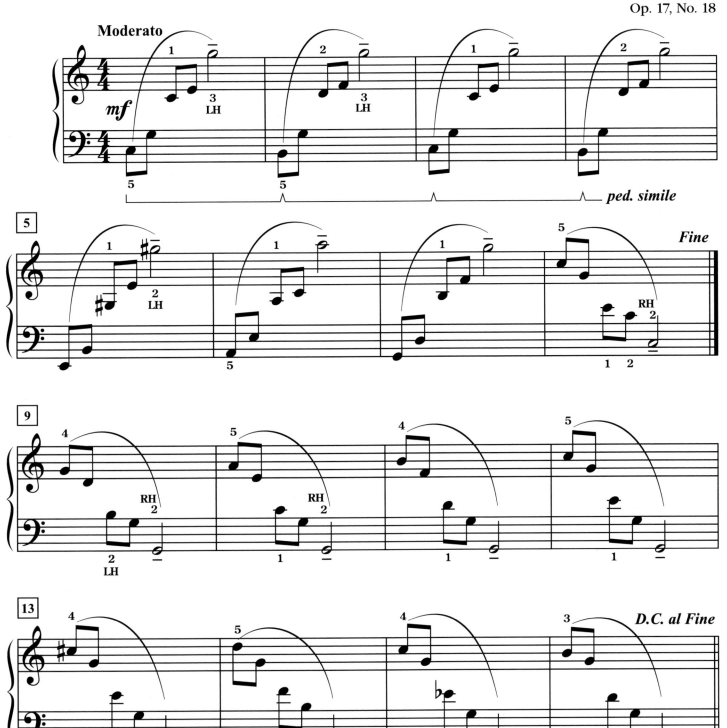

Quadrille, p. 18

Wrist/Hand Staccato

■ Slightly suspend the wrist, keeping the joint loose.

■ **Knock** with a fist on several notes.
Forearm muscles will move the hand from the wrist joint.

■ Keeping **focused fingertips on the keys,** use the same motion to play each finger, rebounding quickly. Play lightly without arm weight.

Play this exercise with a wrist/hand staccato. Fingers should barely move.

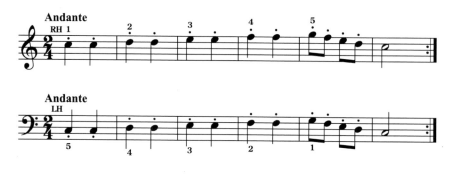

Skipping

Warm-Up Patterns in G

▇ Play mm. 1–3 **three times**, doubling the rhythm on each repeat:
  1) use half notes; 2) quarter notes; 3) eighth notes.

▇ Hold the whole notes throughout each measure (mm. 5–8).

▇ Make a fist to release all staccato chords (mm. 13–15).

▇ Play in minor by lowering the thirds of each pattern.

Five-Finger Patterns in G

- Balance on RH fingers 2, 3 and 4 and LH fingers 3 and 2.
  Hold the whole notes throughout the exercise.

- Slide the thumb under without turning the wrist.

Thumb Slides

- Play scales with the metronome, making the eighth notes exactly twice as fast as the quarters.

- After playing each chord, **relax** the wrist and forearms, keeping the **nail joints firm**.

- First, play hands separately, then together.

G Major and Harmonic Minor Scales with Triads and Inversions

- Play hands separately, LH two octaves lower than written.

- Position the **fingers over the keys** of the pattern **on the first note** of each triplet group.

- Also play in G minor by lowering all B's a half step.

Broken Triads in G

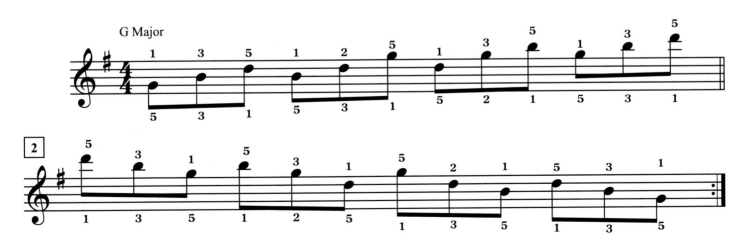

Scale and Four-Note Broken Chord in G

Open the hand over the keys of the four-note broken chords (mm. 2–4).

- After each blocked chord, **relax the knuckles,** keeping the keys down and the **nail joints firm.**
- Play with the RH one octave higher than written.
- Repeat in minor by lowering all B's and E's a half step.

Cadence Workout in G

Two Voices in Both Hands

- **Fall** on the first notes with finger 5 by lowering the suspended wrist to level.

- **Relax** upper arms—then wrists—then knuckles, keeping **firm nail joints**.

- Keep the **weight constant** on fingers 5 when playing the other notes.

- In measure 9, do the same as above, falling and balancing on side tips of fingers 1 (near nail).

- Repeat in G minor by lowering all B's a half step.

Stuck on Five and One

Cornelius Gurlitt (1820–1901)
Op. 82, No. 25

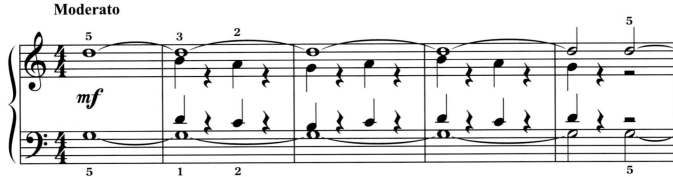

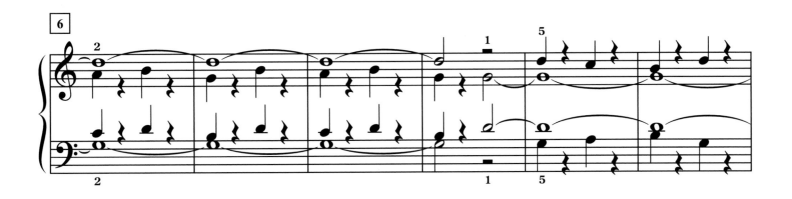

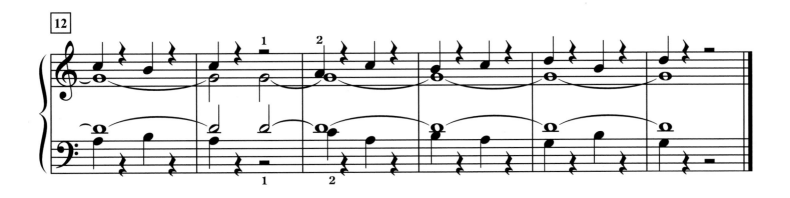

32

Minuet in C Major, p. 22

Rotation

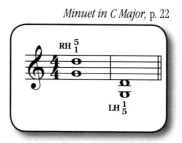

▪ Fall on the interval of a fifth with suspended wrist falling to level. Keeping the nail joints firm, relax the knuckles.

▪ Feel a **connection** between fingers 1 and 5, making an arch through the knuckles.

▪ Keeping the elbow still, **rotate the forearm** (from the elbow)—like turning a doorknob. Keep the upper arm hanging loosely—inactive.

Rotation Etude

Ferdinand Beyer
(1803-1863)

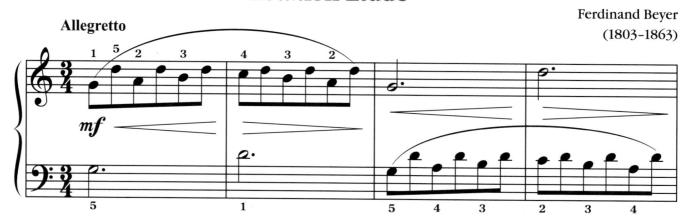

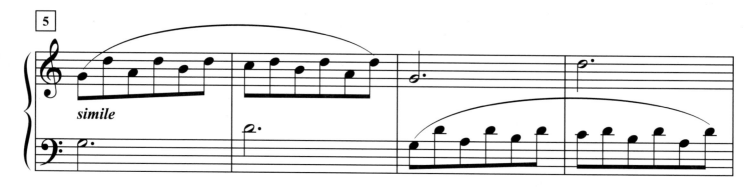

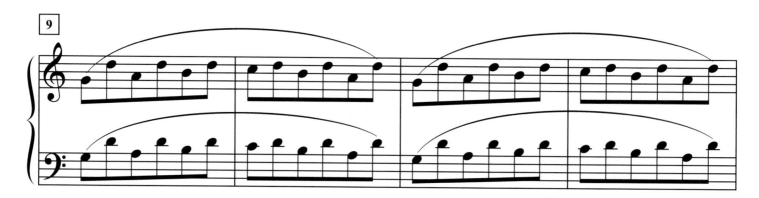

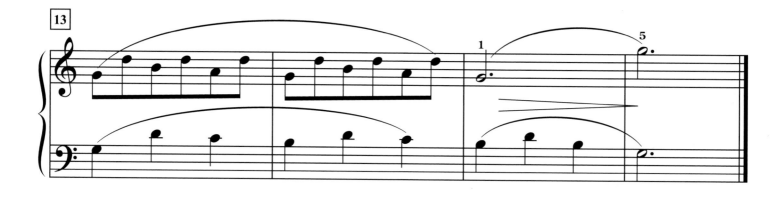

Independent Hands

When playing the piano, the two hands are frequently required to play different touches.

- Sometimes the RH plays legato while the LH plays staccato and vice-versa.

- After playing *Scales with Independence* in D major, as written below, also play it using the C major scale.

Scales with Independence

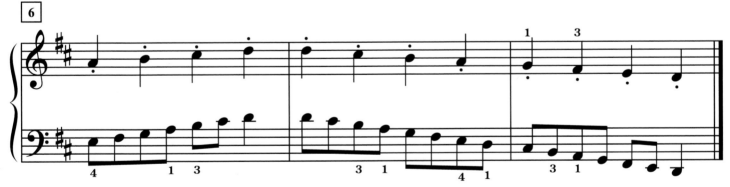

A "Singing" Melody

Sarabande, p. 23

To create a beautiful, singing melodic line:

- Play on the "cushion of flesh" on the first joint, rather than the fingertip.

- Experiment by playing on different parts of the nail joint to create rich tone, shaping the line.

This is a sto - ry that I long to tell.

Minuet in G minor, p. 24

Natural Accents, Slurs, and Motion

$\frac{4}{4}$ time has a strong natural accent on beat 1, and a weaker one on 3:

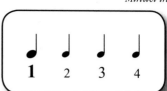

- When the **last note** of a slur group is **on a strong** beat, it receives more fingertip weight, and the line has a **forward motion**.

- Notes without slurs are played detached.

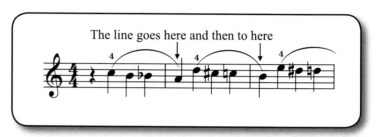

The line goes here and then to here

Moderato

Johann Wilhelm Hässler (1747–1822)
Op. 38, No. 5

Warm-Up Patterns in A

- Play mm. 1–3 **three times**, doubling the rhythm on each repeat:
  1) use half notes; 2) quarter notes; 3) eighth notes.

- Hold the whole notes throughout each measure (mm. 5–8).

- Make a fist to release all staccato chords (mm. 13–15).

- Play in minor by lowering the thirds of each pattern a half step.

Five-Finger Patterns in A

- Balance on RH fingers 2 and 3 and LH fingers 3 and 2.
  Hold the whole notes throughout the exercise.

- Slide the thumb under without turning the wrist.

Thumb Slides

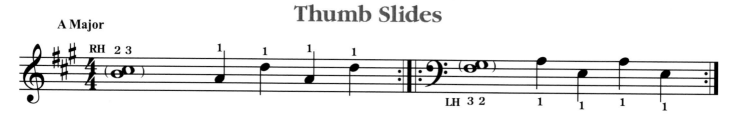

- Play scales with the metronome, making the eighth notes exactly twice as fast as the quarters.

- After playing each chord, **relax** the wrist and forearms, keeping the **nail joints firm**.

- First, play hands separately, then together.

A Major and Harmonic Minor Scales
with Triads and Inversions

Allegro

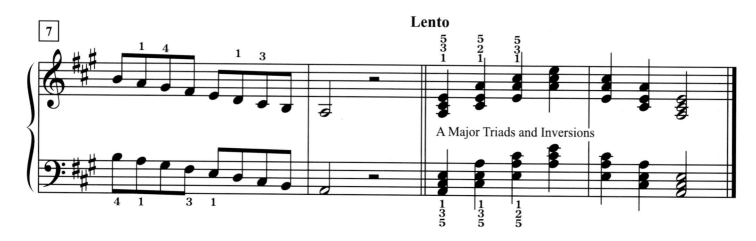

Allegro

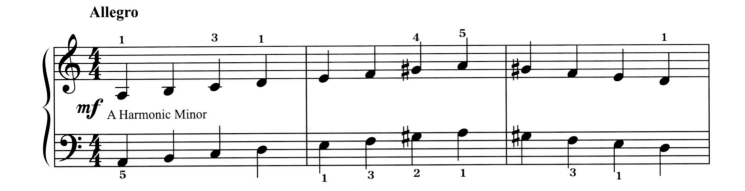

A Harmonic Minor

Lento

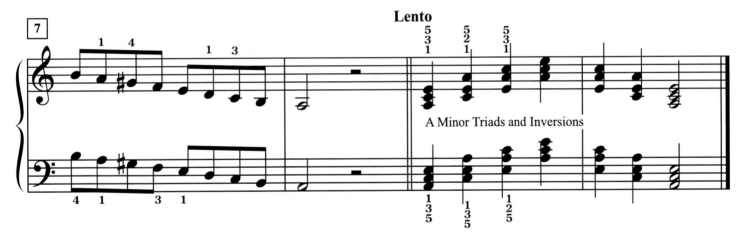

A Minor Triads and Inversions

- Play hands separately, LH two octaves lower than written.

- Position the **fingers over the keys** of the pattern **on the first note** of each triplet group.

- Also play in A minor by lowering all C♯'s a half step.

Broken Triads in A

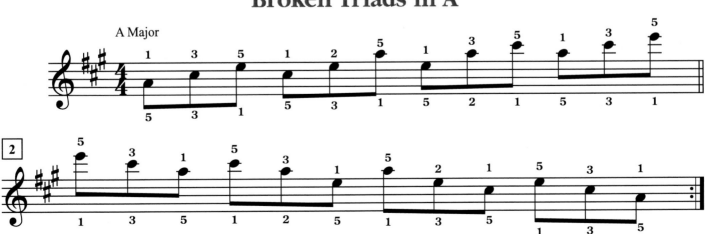

A Major

Scale and Four-Note Broken Chord in A

Open the hand over the keys of the four-note broken chords (mm. 2–4).

- After each blocked chord, **relax the knuckles**, keeping the keys down and the **nail joints firm.**

- Play with the RH one octave higher than written.

- Repeat in minor by lowering all C♯'s and F♯'s a half step.

Cadence Workout in A

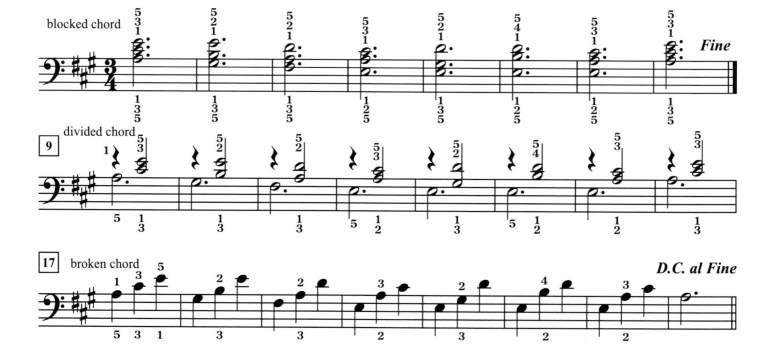

Imitation

▪ In this piece by Gurlitt, the music is the **same in each hand** with the LH following one measure behind the RH until the final cadence of each section. This is know as a **canon**.

▪ Use **slur group touch** for each hand. Practice them hands separately (**fall—transfer—release** touch).

▪ When playing hands together, play each group with **one impulse**.

Canon

Cornelius Gurlitt
(1820–1901)

Russian Folk Song, p. 29

Repeated Chords

A staccato touch is often used for repeated chords, even when not marked with a dot.
The fingertip controls the length of the sound.

■ With fingers on the keys, use a **throwing motion** from the **upper arm** for each measure.

■ Hands and arms should float forward toward the fallboard, while fingers barely move.

■ It should feel like stones **skipping on water.** Practice until comfortable

Bouncing on the Keys

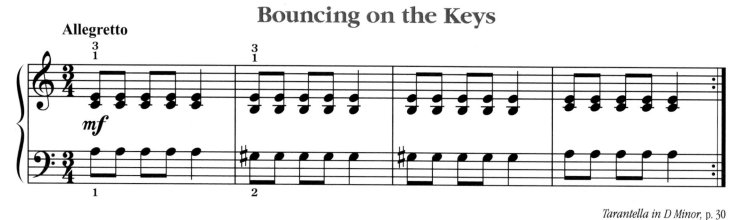

Tarantella in D Minor, p. 30

Chords and Rapid Melodies

One way to increase speed **with control**
is to practice with uneven rhythms.

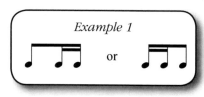

Example 1

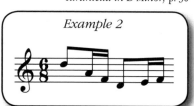

Example 2

■ When the music is in rhythmic groups of three, play the rhythms in Ex. 1.
Relax on the long note (keeping a firm nail joint), and play the short notes quickly.

■ Practice the RH of *Allegro* first with the rhythms in Ex. 2,
then use one throwing motion for each measure when adding LH.

Allegro

Karl Gossec
(1799–1863)

Warm-Up Patterns in E

- Play mm. 1–3 **three times**, doubling the rhythm on each repeat:
  1) use half notes; 2) quarter notes; 3) eighth notes.

- Hold the whole notes throughout each measure (mm. 5–8).

- Make a fist to release all staccato chords (mm. 13–15).

- Play in minor by lowering the thirds of each pattern a half step.

Five-Finger Patterns in E

■ Balance on RH fingers 2 and 3 and LH fingers 3 and 2.
  Hold the whole notes throughout the exercise.

■ Slide the thumb under without turning the wrist.

Thumb Slides

■ Play scales with the metronome, making the eighth notes exactly twice as fast as the quarters.

■ After playing each chord, **relax** the wrist and forearms, keeping the **nail joints firm**.

■ First, play hands separately, then together.

E Major and Harmonic Minor Scales
with Triads and Inversions

- Play hands separately, LH two octaves lower than written.

- Position the **fingers over the keys** of the pattern **on the first note** of each triplet group.

- Also play in E minor by lowering all G's a half step.

Broken Triads in E

Scale and Four-Note Broken Chord in E

Open the hand over the keys of the four-note broken chords (mm. 2–4).

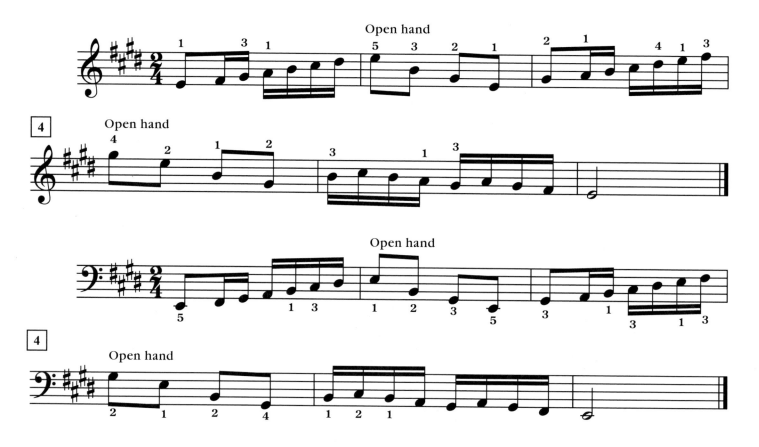

■ After each blocked chord, **relax the knuckles**, keeping the keys down and the **nail joints firm**.

■ Play with the RH one octave higher than written.

■ Repeat in minor by lowering all G♯'s and C♯'s a half step.

Cadence Workout in E

Double Notes

Playing continuous **legato thirds** in one hand **without tension** requires special attention.
One finger must **lead**, or have more weight than the other.

Practice the legato thirds different ways:

▪ First, play the outer fingers (3-4-5) alone.
  Then, add the inner note, keeping the weight in the outer fingers.

▪ After playing each third, **relax knuckles** while keeping firm nail joints.

Play the LH one octave lower.

When playing legato double notes, often a finger must lift when that
same finger moves consecutively, thus breaking the legato connection.

▪ To keep the continuous legato sound, connect the notes with the **changing fingers**
  while lifting the **unchanging finger** at the last second.

Play LH one octave lower. Lift the unchanging finger at the arrows.

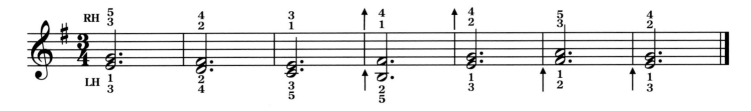

Spanish Dance, p. 34

More Repeated Chords

On the LH repeated chords:

▪ Keeping fingers on the keys, use a **throwing motion** from the upper arm.

▪ Allow the hand and arm to move toward the fallboard with **one motion for each measure.**

Etude in E Major

Felix Le Couppey (1811–1887)
Op. 17, No. 12

Combining Touches

Baroque- and Classical-style keyboard music usually requires
the hands to play different touches at the same time.

■ Release after each slur.

■ Play in D minor on the repeat.

Different Touches

■ For slurs, use one impulse: **fall—transfer—(fingertip) release**.

■ Notes **not** marked legato or staccato, should be played detached.

■ Notes marked with a staccato dot should be played shorter,
with a bouncy sound (pull fingertip back.)

Johann Wilhelm Hässler (1747–1822)
Op. 38, No. 16

Allegro assai

48

Alternating Hands

To play the **intervals with alternating hands**:

▪ Place your fingertips over the keys you are going to play (feeling the key surface).

▪ Bounce from your elbows as though they had springs, with upper arms relaxed.

▪ Give the **accents a special emphasis** with the LH fingertip, and knock on the RH eighth notes.

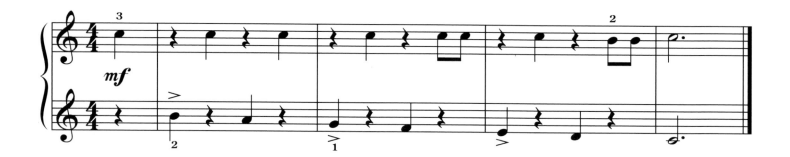

Melody and Ostinato Bass

Peasant Dance, p. 40

Since the human brain can only **think of one thing** at a time, the motions of one hand must become **automatic** when combining different touches.

▪ Play the LH repeated pattern (**ostinato bass**) until it is comfortable, then add the RH.

▪ The LH eighth notes should **lead** or move forward to beat 1 of each measure.

Allegro giocoso